HEARTSTRINGS AT 35,000 FEET

True Stories That Will
Melt Your Heart

Mary Carwile

HEARTSTRINGS AT 35,000 FEET

True Stories That Will
Melt Your Heart

VERBENA POND PUBLISHING
Denver, Colorado

Copyright © 2005 Mary Catherine Carwile

All rights reserved. No part of this book may be used or reproduced in any manner whatsoever without the written permission of the publisher. Printed and bound in the United States of America. For information contact Verbena Pond Publishing Co., LLC, P.O. Box 370270, Denver, Colorado 80237.

First printing 2005

ISBN 09752854-4-0

LCCN 2004116209

Cover and book design: 1106 Design

Dedication

To my husband, Ernie

Without your
love, unconditional support
and never-ending encouragement,
this book would have been
just an unattainable dream.
Thank you, my love.

When you walk to the edge

of all the light you have

and take the first step into the darkness

of the unknown,

you must believe that

one of two things will happen:

There will be something solid

for you to stand upon,

or you will be taught how to fly.

— Patrick Overton
"Faith"

Table of Contents

Preface 11

Acknowledgements 13

Row One 17

Precious Cargo..25

The Bracelet..31

The Bracelet: Part Two 37

More Than Just a Diamond 43

She Earned Her Wings.....................................49

Heartstrings at 35,000 Feet • Mary Catherine Carwile

We Never Know 55

The Christmas Gift 61

The Little Girl Nobody Wanted............................67

His Name Was John 73

Things Aren't Always What They Seem..................81

A Time To Live and a Time To Die......................87

Angels Watching Over Me 93

Protect the Children 99

Precious Cargo: The Rest of the Story.................107

A Rose Is a Rose 113

Ross's Story: You Knew..119

No Ordinary Day...121

Preface

"When you come to the edge of all you've known and are about to step into darkness, one of two things will happen: There will be something solid for you to stand on or you will be taught to fly." I'd heard that somewhere but never having been a big risk taker, I didn't find much meaning in it at the time. Several years later, it came to have real meaning to me. Coming out of a divorce and surviving breast cancer taught me that I shouldn't take the bumps in the road too seriously. I'd also heard that something that doesn't kill you makes you stronger. Well, dying wasn't an option. I didn't know, however, what my next step would be. Should I move? Should I find a new career? When someone suggested I apply to become a flight attendant, I laughed! "Are you kidding me?" was all I could say, what with my fear of flying and of being in closed spaces. Well, as it happened, I walked to the edge of all I knew and stepped off.

To my great relief, the universe smiled upon me. I was

given a chance and taught to fly. I earned my wings. I *did* become a flight attendant—in my midfifties, no less. I wear my wings proudly.

My life has taken on a whole new meaning now. While I love being a flight attendant, I've found that conversations with passengers have been the highlight of most days on the job. The reception one passenger's story received when I shared it with guests at dinner parties led me to write this book. They were always moved by this passenger's experience and asked to hear more stories like it.

This book contains experiences told to me while flying some thirty-five thousand feet above the earth. The reasons people fly are many. There are holidays, cruises and weddings. There are also funerals, divorces and illnesses. Passengers may be happy, sad, anxious—in fact, many people are simply afraid to fly. It's amazing how people open up and want to talk to a stranger.

You will find these stories meaningful, thought provoking and inspiring. Each reading may evoke a memory or spark lost feelings hiding deep within your heart. You may see yourself, your loved ones, your co-workers or friends within a story.

My hope is that the stories in this book will touch your heart as they have touched mine.

Acknowledgements

I have collected the stories in this book over a span of the few years I have been working in the airline industry. They were taken in most cases from my conversations with passengers.

A couple of the stories were taken from conversations with flight attendants and are retellings of their experiences with passengers. I have chosen to write these in the first person as they were told to me.

To my fellow flight attendants, thank you for sharing your stories with me. I look forward to "seeing you upstairs" in the near future.

I want to thank all the passengers who trusted me enough to speak to me and share their intimate stories with me. Being confined in an aircraft traveling at five hundred miles per hour at thirty-five thousand feet does make one believe that we're all in this together. I hope my stories touch readers and let them know that we are, indeed, all part of the same, beautiful world. Love and sharing certainly bridge the gap of fear.

Thank you, my two precious sons, Ross and Cole. My heart swells with pride at the mention of your names. You are the joy in my life, the love in my heart. I appreciate your continuing support. There were times when you parented me. Now we're *all* spreading our wings.

Kate, my sweet stepdaughter, you are a delight in my life. Thank you for your suggestions, ideas and encouragement.

Thanks to Jeff Mlady and Joyce Miller, my editors, for your editing expertise. Jeff, you gave me such a needed boost of confidence by loving my book from the very beginning. Joyce, your research and your suggestions as the writing progressed were invaluable.

Cathy Shuster, my virtual assistant, you are always there with enthusiastic words of encouragement and support. Thanks!

Honesty is the first chapter

in the book of wisdom.

— Thomas Jefferson

Row One

The older couple caught my eye as they boarded the plane. They had the routine down, the way they took care of each other. I guessed they were in their seventies.

While I continued the boarding process, I could see out of the corner of my eye how she helped him find his seat, how he held her small bag until she was seated. There was just something about them.

After takeoff, I began the beverage service. I'm always thrilled when our flights aren't too full. That way I have more time to interact with the passengers.

Such was this flight from Tampa to Denver. As I approached the elderly couple in row one and offered them drinks, I inquired, "Are you going to Denver for a visit, or is Denver home?"

The woman looked up at me, half smiled, and said, "Oh no, we're going to a funeral."

Heartstrings at 35,000 Feet • Mary Catherine Carwile

"I'm so sorry," was all I could say just then. I noticed the man wore a tag that read LEGALLY BLIND and wondered to myself, *how much sight does he have?* I handed them their drinks.

The gentleman smiled and said in a voice full of spunk, "My name is Nathaniel. This is Katherine. We just go by Nate and Kate." We all laughed, and with that, Nate and Kate became my buddies.

When I finished the beverage service and had a few minutes to spare, I leaned down to chat again with Nate and Kate. They were delightful, and I felt comfortable with them immediately.

On a late-night flight a few months before, one wide-awake passenger had shown me how to make paper roses out of our cocktail napkins. Thinking Kate might like a rose, I slipped into the galley to make one, popped my head around the bulkhead, and presented it to her. You'd have thought I'd given her a real, live, red rose.

"Oh! Show me how to do that, won't you?" she exclaimed.

So Kate (and Nate) got a very quick instructional lesson on paper rose making. I left them with several napkins while I went back to work. Upon my return to row one, I saw not one, but two nearly perfect paper roses.

"Look! And Nate made his without much help from me at all . . . remember he is legally blind!" After that, our conversation was pretty much continuous with only short breaks while I worked the flight.

As I walked past my newfound friends, Kate, with a twinkle in her eyes, said, "We're about to celebrate our fiftieth!"

Row One

"I'm so jealous," I said. "I'm divorced and in my fifties; I doubt that I'll ever see a fiftieth wedding anniversary."

She smiled and, with her eyes just dancing, said, "Oh, I didn't say fifty years, sweetheart. We're celebrating fifty *months!*" We laughed and then embarked on a fun conversation on love and romance.

After answering a passenger call light in row sixteen, I returned to row one, anticipating more enjoyable chatter. Kate inquired about my life a bit, and I shared exciting news that I had met the man of my dreams just a few weeks before, also on a flight from Florida. That flight, too, was only half full. I'd struck up a conversation with a very handsome gentleman seated in the emergency exit row. I recounted the story of that meeting—how we chatted about his reason for going to Denver (he lives there) and what he did for a living.

"I promise," I told Nate and Kate, "I was simply being a friendly flight attendant. Nothing else . . . just yet. But back to the story . . . When the man in the emergency exit row said he was a writer . . . I have to tell you, my heart skipped a beat.

"I told him my son, Ross, was a writer too, and we embarked on a conversation about writing books and anecdotes . . . then I remembered I had a very special piece that Ross had written. I always carry it with me in my flight bag. I asked him if he would like to read it. He said he would love to. What else did he have to do for three more hours?" I laughed.

I went on to tell them the rest of the story—how the man I'd met that day did indeed become the man of my dreams and how we are happy-ever-aftering. Kate asked if I still carry the piece Ross wrote. "But, of course. Would you like to read it, too?"

"We'd be honored."

I gave the story to Kate and walked away, but I heard her voice behind me, so I turned. She was sitting up close to her Nate reading the story to him.

Later I returned to row one. Nate and Kate said they both loved the story.

Just then, Nate got up to use the lavatory. I slipped into his seat for a brief moment off my feet. What happened next still haunts me.

While sitting next to Kate, I shared with her the impact Ross's story had on my new love and the fact that he told me some intimate details of his life. I explained, "He told me that he'd been badly abused by his father . . . "

Kate's sudden gasp surprised me and I stared at her.

"Are you okay?"

She looked down and quietly said, "I had something bad happen to me as a child, too."

I waited.

She continued. "When I was eight years old my mother and father called me and my three sisters into the parlor. With her finger pointing at each of us she said, 'One of you took a quarter from my coin purse. Which one of you did it?' I was the first to speak up. 'Mama, I didn't take your quarter. Papa, I did not take Mama's quarter!'

"They didn't believe me. They took me into their bedroom and beat me, hard, with a spatula. I turned all black and blue."

Row One

At this point, Kate touched me at my waist and just below to show me where the bruises had colored her small body.

"Many years later, when I was twenty years old, I said to my mother, 'Mama, remember when I was eight years old and you accused me of stealing a quarter from your coin purse? Well, Mama, I didn't take it!'

"Mama just looked at me and said, 'Oh, Katherine. You know you did!'"

After all this time, I thought, *it still matters to her!*

"When I was older I was visiting my sister. I said to her, 'Elizabeth, remember when we were kids and Mama accused me of stealing a quarter? Well, Elizabeth, I didn't take the quarter!'

"Elizabeth just laughed. She said, 'I know you didn't, Katherine. I did!'"

The silence between us hung in the air, but the sound of the airplane engines seemed very loud. Neither Kate nor I spoke for a few moments. Finally I said to her, "Kate, was your mother still alive at that time?"

"Yes."

I leaned forward, stretching to look at her face, searching her eyes. "Did you tell her?" I asked.

Kate's reply gave me goose bumps.

"No. I was too embarrassed for Elizabeth."

I couldn't speak! *Too embarrassed for Elizabeth?* I thought.

And then Kate said solemnly, "That's whose funeral I'm going to tomorrow."

Not flesh of my flesh

nor bone of my bone,

but still miraculously my own.

Never forget for a single minute:

You didn't grow under my heart,

but in it!

— Author unknown

Precious Cargo

I wonder how they felt when the telephone rang early that morning.

"We have a baby for you!" They had heard this before. It had been less than a year since they had received an identical message.

Thrilled, they'd made arrangements, and in less than a week were on their way around the globe. Vietnam. Just the name evokes memories of the war and its inescapable images. But that was another time. This time Vietnam represented a mission of love. They were going to get a baby of their own.

Sadly, it did not play out that way. Only days after they arrived in the hot, humid country, their tiny daughter fell ill with measles and died.

Flying home empty-handed was almost more than they could bear.

But, now there was hope. Hope that maybe this time there could be a family. Hope that this time the small boy would be theirs to love, to raise, to cherish.

"The baby will be arriving in San Francisco the day after tomorrow," they were told by their adoption agency. "Someone will call you. They will tell you where to pick up your baby. Good luck."

Adoption agencies sometimes use airline personnel to transport this precious cargo. It proves too costly for new parents to purchase last-minute tickets.

I, too, got a call.

"We just got the word," she said to me. "A six-month-old Korean boy is being flown to the United States. His new parents live in Denver. Can you fly to San Fran on Monday?"

"Of course I can!" I nearly shouted into the phone.

So it was that I found myself at international customs in San Francisco.

Searching the crowd, I spotted a couple of women with babies, but didn't know for sure which baby was my charge. I noticed one young woman carrying a baby in a front pack. She and the child looked so comfortable together, yet she seemed to be searching the crowd, too.

That can't be the woman I'm looking for, I said to myself. She was so serene, calm and loving that I just assumed she was the birth mother.

But, she moved toward me and I knew that, indeed, she was the one.

After presenting the proper identification papers, we exchanged introductions, hugs, and a few instructions.

Then I was left on my own to deliver six-month-old Tae to his new mom and dad.

Nearly three hours before our flight left for Denver, little Tae—soon to be renamed Owen—and I found a nice quiet spot in an airport café. I entertained him, he entertained me, and together we found that little Owen loved yogurt. *Had he tasted it in Korea?* I wondered.

After having flown for nearly twenty-four hours, he was still all smiles and giggles. A real trouper, he was. While in the boarding area, Owen, strapped to my chest, finally found a safe and comfortable place to sleep. And sleep he did.

While he dozed, I visited with a gentleman also flying to Denver. He was a sportscaster from Kansas City and had been in San Francisco filming an event. His crew's large camera rested on the floor. As we waited together, he learned why this middle-aged woman had a small baby on her chest, and I learned that he had two children of his own . . . both adopted. *A coincidence?*

"Do you think it would be all right for me to get off the airplane before you?" he asked. "I'd love to film you handing the baby to his new parents." He quickly added, "With their permission, of course."

Without a moment's hesitation, I replied, "Great idea." What a wonderful surprise it would be for this new family. They would have forever on film the moment they first laid eyes on each other.

The main cabin door opened and we were out—the sportscaster, the baby, and me.

The captain had called ahead to order an electric cart

for us. We had to hurry, as the sportscaster needed to make a connecting flight to Kansas City. As we rode to our meeting place at the security checkpoint, his camera rolled. The baby was very sleepy, yet happy and smiling. I whispered to Owen that he was about to meet his mom and dad.

"All will be well, Owen," I said soothingly. "You are in America now, and life will be good."

As we crested the sky bridge and headed down the other side, I heard joyful screams.

"Oh, my God, there he is. He's beautiful . . . " Owen's new mom had just seen her son.

The emotions I had planned to keep in check broke loose. With tears streaming down my face, I handed over that precious baby boy.

Owen, his mom, his dad, and I hugged for the longest time.

For just a brief moment, I felt like God.

The best thing about the future is that

it only comes one day at a time.

– Abraham Lincoln

The Bracelet

I'd had it only a few hours. The bracelet was such a find. With just a few hours remaining on my layover, I knew I would be back in uniform and flying again by mid-afternoon. But, I decided to spend the time browsing the shops at the harbor in Baltimore. It was there the piece had caught my eye. It was unusual. It just spoke to me.

The black stone was beautiful. What held it together—actually made it a bracelet—was the fork. The utensil had been twisted and bent, forming a unique bracelet. I might have missed it, had it not been for the sign that hung above it: THE FORK LADY.

It had such special meaning to me. A couple of years before, a story had been told by my pastor in a very moving sermon.

❤ ❤ ❤

You see, some time ago there was a woman, very ill and near death, who had summoned her pastor to her side. Having accepted the inevitable, she was ready to put her affairs in order. Her funeral was to be "a celebration, not a serious occasion." She made that clear.

"Young man," she began, "I want to wear my new blue dress, the one with tiny flowers on it. And," she continued, "make sure they do my hair right!" She was a feisty one.

She told him what songs should be sung, what scripture had been comforting to her, and what kind of flowers should adorn the church altar. But her last request startled the young pastor.

"Oh, and one more thing. Make sure there is a fork in my right hand."

Did he hear her correctly? "Mrs. Cartwright, did you say to place a *fork* in your hand?"

"I certainly did," she said, her eyes twinkling.

The old woman had his attention.

"You see," she began, "when I was a small girl, my mama and daddy used to take me to church. Every so often, we'd have a dinner after church—a potluck, you know. The food was wonderful, and there were always new and mouthwatering surprises. Well, don't you know, towards the end of the meal one of the nice ladies would always come by to take away my dirty plate."

She smiled broadly as the memories took over.

"Because the desserts were about to be brought out, she would lean over and whisper, 'Hang on to your fork, young lady. The best is yet to come.'

The Bracelet

"That's the message I want to leave my friends," she said. "It's a good one, don't you think?"

The pastor was moved to tears. Her wishes would indeed be granted.

♥ ♥ ♥

That story had real meaning to me when, shortly after I heard the story, I was diagnosed with breast cancer.

The doctors told me it had been caught early. Surgery, with some time to heal, and I'd be fine, they said.

My marriage was ending, too. Great timing.

I needed something positive to cling to; so that fork story kept coming to mind. *Is the best yet to come?* I found myself asking.

On Christmas Eve, just a few months after surgery, I was with my two grown sons. Living in a mountain resort community, we'd just returned from the annual torchlight ski-down. It was beautiful but sad in that melancholy Christmas way. We had to rush home, change clothes and head for church. I was singing in the choir, and there wasn't much time.

"I'm sorry, guys," I said to my boys through my tears. "I hate feeling so sad, but this has just been a tough year for me."

Ross, my eldest, said, "Oh, don't worry, Mom. The best is yet to come." I smiled and sensed his wisdom.

Singing "Silent Night" with only everyone's handheld candles lighting the church was a perfect end to the service. It brought back, however, those lonely feelings again.

Once home, we exchanged our Christmas gifts. As I opened the gift from Ross, I was filled with hope and the

Heartstrings at 35,000 Feet • Mary Catherine Carwile

true Christmas spirit. For inside that tiny box, gleamed a sterling silver baby fork. On the handle was engraved MOM, THE BEST IS YET TO COME.

Love and kindness are never wasted.

They always make a difference.

They bless the one who receives them,

and they bless you, the giver.

— Barbara DeAngelis

The Bracelet: Part Two

That bracelet took on a life of its own!

I was proudly wearing my special bracelet just hours after I'd spotted it at the little shop in Baltimore. It was special to *me*, I knew, but I didn't expect it to speak to anyone else.

Working the flight back to Denver, we three attendants were having fun. During the safety demonstration, the flight attendant in the rear of the plane laughingly said, "Tonight your flight attendants from front to back are Mary Sunshine, Dianne Daffodil, and I'm Mary Quite Contrary."

Sunshine—well, actually Little Mary Sunshine—had been my childhood nickname. Mary Quite Contrary decided to add a little humor in the all-too-familiar "this is your seat belt" demonstration.

Well, this time it worked. The passengers laughed along with us. It seemed like there weren't many attendant call buttons impatiently pushed that night.

While working the cabin, not one, not two, but *many* people asked me about my beautiful and unique bracelet.

"I just bought it today," I'd say.

Then I'd show them how the bracelet was actually made out of an old fork. It was a beautifully twisted silver fork with a large black stone. I'd bend down and let them get a good look at my special bracelet.

One lady talked with me a bit longer than the rest. She and I had several short conversations during the flight. She told me that she calls her little grandson "Robbie Sunshine," and we shared a laugh together. She asked about my bracelet, too. Something inside told me to share the fork story with her.

We never know what impact we have on people. Being onboard an airplane, people often say things to us that they wouldn't normally say to a stranger. Maybe it's a feeling that we're all in it together. Maybe it's a comfort to talk to someone while flying through the dark skies. I don't know.

That night was just rather special, though.

When I stood at the front of the plane sending people off with a "Goodnight, now," or "Thanks for flying with us tonight," the grandmother I'd spoken to several times during the flight pressed a small note into my hand.

After all the passengers deplaned, I had a moment to look at the note I was still holding in my hand. It read:

Dear Mary,
When the attendant announced your name as Mary Sunshine, I felt a strong impulse to tell you about my grandson, whose nickname from me is "Robbi Sunshine" because he is the sunshine of my life. Your

The Bracelet: Part Two

story about the fork was inspired. I have, in the last few months, lost hope of anything in my life going right, and Robbie Sunshine was and is the only light I could see at the end of this tunnel I feel I'm in. I feel your story was meant to be shared with me in particular because for so long I have felt the best was over.

Thank you, Mary Sunshine
I look forward to the best that's
yet to come in my life.

We were just strangers passing in the night, but I won't forget her. I trust she won't forget me. Every time either of us sees a fork, we'll remember and know, *the best is yet to come.*

Love and marriage, love and marriage,

go together like a horse and carriage.

Dad was told by Mother

you can't have one . . . without the other.

— Sammy Cahn

More Than Just a Diamond

We don't see hats anymore. Not like we used to. I remember when I was in college; a hat was *required attire* for attending church on Sundays.

I was boarding the passengers early one day, greeting each one with a cheerful "Good Morning!" One small, older woman caught my eye. She wasn't five feet tall. She was small in stature, but I could tell right away she had spunk. She was dressed "properly," the way people *used* to dress to fly in an airplane. She might have been going to church. Her simple, tailored suit was flattering and gave her an air of, well, importance. Her shoes and handbag matched, of course. But what really made her stand out from the rest was her hat. It, too, matched. It made the outfit complete.

After asking for help to place her carry-on bag in the overhead bin, she settled into her aisle seat. She had a book to read, complete with a handmade, floral-cloth cover.

She'd even brought her own lunch. She knew one couldn't always rely on the airlines to provide a balanced lunch anymore. She had a banana, a sandwich, and three chocolate chip cookies that she had packed in a small, brown paper bag.

About halfway through the flight, I saw her checking on each side of her seat, apparently looking for something. I asked her if she'd lost anything.

"Oh dear," she said, rather embarrassed. "I seem to have lost my diamond ring."

As I helped her look for the ring, she explained, "The ring was very important to me. You see, it was my grandmother's ring. She gave it to my mother, and my mother passed it down to me. It really isn't that big, and I'm sure it isn't worth much money, but it is worth so much to the family. I'm going to my granddaughter's wedding tomorrow. It's her turn to wear the ring now. Oh, I feel so silly!"

The passengers in the seats nearby overheard her tell the story. Everyone seemed to want to help her find her ring. Several people got out of their seats, got on their knees and looked under the seats, in the aisle, and in the seatback pockets.

No ring.

My flying partner and I had already collected two large bags of trash from the beverage and snack service.

"Would you like me to search the trash bags and see if it was thrown away somehow?" I asked her.

I knew she wasn't one to ask that of anyone, but I could see the panic in her eyes.

"Oh sweetie, would you mind?" was all she had to say.

With rubber-gloved hands, I took every single piece of trash out of those bags. I found lots of stuff . . . but no ring.

"Well, you tried," she said sadly.

Sitting in her seat now, she looked even smaller. And she was so sad. What would she tell her granddaughter? This "something old" was lost forever.

I was still trying to think of some words to cheer her up as we ran through the cabin one last time, filling another large bag with the last of the empty soda cans and coffee cups. Then just minutes before we were to land, as I passed by her aisle seat, she placed a small, brown lunch bag into the trash.

When I returned to the galley, I opened the brown bag. *Maybe, just maybe,* I thought. There was one banana peel, two pieces of balled-up clear plastic wrap—*and one small, shiny diamond ring.*

"I found it! I found it!" I shouted.

Everyone cheered and clapped as I walked to her and placed the precious ring in her hand.

Through tears of gratitude she said, "I'm nearly ninety years old. You've made me a very happy old lady today."

I'm sure the wedding went off as planned. I'm not sure if she told her granddaughter about temporarily loosing the ring. I guess it didn't matter much. The ring was now in her care. She could pass it on to her daughter one day.

> *Something old*
> Something new
> *Something borrowed*
> Something blue

Heartstrings at 35,000 Feet • Mary Catherine Carwile

I've heard that old adage all my life. But now, it means so much more.

The pain passes, but the beauty remains.

— Pierre Auguste Renoir

She Earned Her Wings

When they got up from their seats, I quickly got on the PA to remind them the seat belt sign was still illuminated and that it wasn't safe to move about the cabin just yet. The mother and little girl continued their walk toward the back of the airplane.

"They never listen to us," I huffed under my breath to my flying partner Burt.

As they approached us in the galley, the mom said, "I'm so sorry. She just can't wait. We'll be very careful!"

Burt and I were in the back galley preparing the cart for the beverage service. It was a short flight to Omaha, and there wasn't much time to get everything organized, the people served, and the galley cleaned and locked up. Having this little girl and her mom in our way didn't make it any easier. Just then, this blue-eyed seven-year-old asked, "Hey, Mister, can I have those wings?" as she looked up at Burt, hopefully, through incredibly long eyelashes.

Heartstrings at 35,000 Feet • Mary Catherine Carwile

"Hey!" Burt said with humor in his voice. Then he got down to her level and said, "These wings were very hard to get. I had to go to weeks of flight attendant training. I had to memorize tons of stuff. I had to learn how to use a fire extinguisher . . . "

She was standing on one foot, then the other. Those blue eyes screamed, *Mom, I have to go.*

Burt caught the drift. "Oh sorry, sweetie," he apologized.

As the cute little girl slipped into the small lavatory, her mom explained to Burt and me, "I'm sorry she's bothering you. She just loves airplanes. I guess she thought having your wings would just make her day."

And then she added, "Brittney has cancer. They've told us she doesn't have long to live. We just returned from Disneyland. It was a Make A Wish trip. Brittney rode on every ride they had. She saw Mickey and Minnie and Goofy. Honestly, she had a ball. Although she got really tired, she refused to quit."

I felt as if my heart leapt to my throat. I glanced at Burt. His eyes were suddenly really big.

Just then Brittney opened the lavatory door. Burt turned aside and quickly wiped away the tears, and then he again bent down to her level.

"Hey Brittney," he said, "I think you need these wings after all." He took them off his uniform and pinned them on her little shirt. It was then that we noticed. Under her brightly colored Minnie Mouse hat, Brittney had no hair.

It didn't matter how hard Burt had worked for his wings. Brittney *deserved* those wings!

Her mom asked Burt for his address. He took hers, too.

50

She Earned Her Wings

He told her if there was anything—*anything*—he could do to help, please call him.

One day about four months later, Burt told me he had gotten a letter the day before. It was postmarked from Brittney's city. He told me how excited he had been and how he had quickly torn it open, expecting to see a picture colored by little Brittney. Instead, he said, he read her mom's words, "We lost our beautiful baby last week. We thought you'd want to know."

Burt tried to hold back his emotions, but he just couldn't. With tears streaming down his cheeks, he repeated for me the last line of the letter. "She wore your wings every single day!"

How far you go in life depends on

your being tender with the young,

compassionate with the aged,

sympathetic with the striving

and tolerant of the weak and strong.

Because someday in life you will

have been all of these.

– George Washington Carver

We Never Know

My fellow flight attendant motioned to me from the back galley. "That lady in 20F wants to be moved. She doesn't want to sit with the baby," she said to me, her voice reflecting annoyance toward the female passenger.

The plane was nearly full, but I knew there were a few empty seats located near the front of the plane. It wouldn't be a problem to move the woman. Something inside prompted me to avoid taking on the annoyed attitude of the other flight attendant.

Leaning over a young man holding a small infant, I said to the anxious-to-move woman, "Would you like to have a seat up closer to the front of the plane?" Her look told me she was a bit embarrassed and didn't want to make a fuss. It also told me she was most relieved to be changing seats.

I'd seen the young family board. They had three children between them. Mom took the two small girls and sat across the aisle from Dad and the new baby. It always warms my heart when I see dads caring for small children. So often that job falls to the mother. Our society seems to dictate that only mothers have been given the nurturing gene. But I've witnessed too many occasions proving that's not true at all.

When the woman passenger excused herself to exit the row, the young father looked hurt. The baby wasn't even crying. *Why does she want to move away from us?* he must have wondered.

I didn't understand either, but wanting to please, I obliged and walked her forward to row four.

Just before she sat down in her new seat, the woman looked at me with such concern in her eyes. She put one hand up by her mouth so as not to be heard by the passengers nearby.

"I don't mean to be rude," she whispered. "I hope you don't think I'm awful . . . wanting to move away from the baby."

"Of course not," I replied, although I didn't really understand.

Do we ever really know why some passengers are angry, sad, excited, or frightened? The reasons people choose to fly are as varied as the people themselves.

But this woman had an explanation that left me speechless. "You see, I just lost my grandbaby. I'm going home to his funeral. I just couldn't sit by that adorable baby. You understand . . . "

I had to fight to hold back my tears. *Now it makes sense,* I thought. It wasn't that she did not want to be bothered by a crying baby the entire flight. Not at all.

We Never Know

I rushed back to row twenty to tell the young father. He was moved and grateful. Every time I passed by his row during that flight, I saw him looking into his baby's eyes. I *know* he'll never look at his children the same way he did before that flight.

Blessed is the season which

engages the whole world

in a conspiracy of love.

– Hamilton Wright Mabie

The Christmas Gift

It was Christmas Day, and I was working. Not exactly what I had in mind. *Who flies on Christmas Day?* I wondered.

I was surprised to find that *lots* of people fly on Christmas Day. I suppose the reasons are as varied as the faces I saw while boarding the airplane on that early morning flight.

I was all decked out with Christmas pins on my blazer and even a reindeer headband. Everyone made some comment as they saw me.

"Where's your red nose?"

"Does it light up?"

"Are you guiding the plane tonight?"

It made the mood festive and fun.

The plane was full, and it was difficult finding enough overhead bin space in which to place all the bags and coats, to say nothing about the volume of brightly wrapped gifts.

As I walked through the cabin one last time before take-off, I noticed a young father and his small son sitting in a row together. The little guy was fastened into his car seat, excitedly looking out the window. Dad was pointing to other aircraft on the runway as the little boy's voice echoed through the cabin, "Airplane, Daddy, airplane!"

I wondered, as I sat on the jump seat, *Just where is the mother? It is Christmas Day, after all.*

Once we were able to start our beverage service, I walked past the pair again. It was a sight that warmed my heart. Dad was fast asleep with his head resting against the small car seat. The little man was all eyes, taking in everyone and everything, but not uttering a word.

During our beverage service, I handed a soft drink to a very pregnant woman near the rear of the aircraft. We chatted a minute before she said, "Do you suppose you could help me with my heavy bag when we land? My husband put it up for me, and I just can't get it down alone."

I told her I'd be happy to help her and then asked, "But where is your husband now?"

"Oh, he's sitting up near the front."

I thought their seating arrangements strange, but didn't have time for more conversation right then.

By the third trip through the cabin, I had put two and two together. Walking past her again, I stopped at her row and asked her if, by chance, her husband was sitting with a small boy.

"Yes," she replied with a smile.

I couldn't figure out the separate seating, and it kept nagging me.

The Christmas Gift

"In case you're wondering," I said as I approached her again, "your husband is sound asleep, and your darling little boy is wide-awake, watching everything that is going on."

"Oh man," she said with a laugh, "that baby is always so good for his dad!"

Just a few minutes before we were preparing to land, I noticed the dad was awake. I also noticed that the seat next to him was still empty, as it had been the entire flight.

"I told your wife that you had a good nap," I said, goodheartedly.

He laughed and then added, "Is she okay?"

"Oh, she's fine. But . . . if you don't mind my asking . . . why isn't she sitting next to you."

His eyes lit up, and with much love in his voice, he said, "Oh, this is my Christmas gift to her."

I knew just what he meant. She was going to have two hours—two full hours—to sit alone. She could sleep. She could read. She could do nothing, but she did not have to worry about her son. She was soon to have another child, and time alone was precious. I know. I'm a mom, too.

Christmas gifts usually come wrapped in beautiful, shiny paper topped with a huge bow—usually, but not always.

O Great Spirit,

grant that I may never judge another

until I have walked

a mile in his moccasins.

— Old Indian proverb

The Little Girl
Nobody Wanted

Walk a mile in his shoes. That is the only way to truly know how someone else feels, reacts, or makes choices. People choose different paths for different reasons—reasons as varied as the people themselves. Terminating a pregnancy could be one choice, choosing to give away your child, quite another.

As the couple boarded the plane, I smiled at the darling little girl the man carried in his arms. "I love your red shoes," I said to her as she passed by me.

"Say thank you, Willow," the older woman chided the child.

I assumed she and the man must be the girl's grandparents. Both their age and the difference between their features and those of the baby led me to believe they were not biological parents. Her coal black hair and her beautiful dark skin definitely were not a match to their Caucasian features. They moved on to search for their seats, and I didn't see them again until I served them beverages.

"Oh, I do apologize," the grandmother said to me. "Really, she's usually just an angel." Little Willow had found her voice and was screaming at the top of her lungs. I had heard her as we were taxiing before takeoff. "We thought it would be such a great idea to take Willow to see her new aunt, uncle and five cousins, but now I'm not so sure."

"Can I see those red shoes again?" I asked the little screamer. That's all it took. She was all ears and smiles.

As I examined her tiny red slippers, I had a chance to continue my talk with the grandparents. "Tell me about little Willow," I inquired.

"Well, she's the little girl nobody wanted. Can you imagine?"

I could not. A child is such a gift from God. How could anyone not want this perfect, beautiful little person? But not all situations allow a brand-new baby girl.

"How did she come to you? What happened?" I was full of questions.

The grandmother was eager to share. "My daughter teaches at a school for the deaf. One of the young men attending school was escorted to school often by his older sister. She was only nineteen years old, yet she was the mother of two children. It wasn't long before it became apparent she was about to have her third child."

I tried to imagine how hard that would be. Having children and supporting and loving them can be trying in the best of circumstances, but for a mother so young, without a good job or proper support—well, it can't be easy.

"My daughter talked with the young pregnant woman often when she dropped off her brother for school. She must have felt very safe with my daughter. She obviously trusted her."

The little screamer was at it again. I guess I wasn't paying enough attention to her. "Hey, little one, tell me your name," I said to her. Of course I knew her name was Willow, but my question diverted her attention once again.

Her grandma laughed and said, "Well, her full name is Willow Speak Thunder. That's her Native American name."

"Perfect," I said with a smile. "She is already living up to that name. But, tell me more. How did she end up with you?"

"Well, the young mother didn't come to school for a week or so. When she did return, she carried a tiny bundle in her arms. The baby was dressed in just a diaper and a thin blanket, even though it was so cold outside."

The mental image tore at my heart. I thought how most people take so much for granted.

"The young mother asked my daughter, 'Will you keep her for just a few days?' Well, one day turned into two and then into weeks. My daughter already had a family. Her two boys were eleven and fourteen, but she took on that baby with open arms and an open heart. Her husband loved the infant the moment his eyes met hers, and from then on it was a done deal. They were going to make that baby part of their family."

"Did your daughter ever see the mother again?" I asked.

"Oh yes. She comes to the school every so often. Usually to inquire how little Willow is doing. She just can't raise another child. And you know, it is very difficult to adopt

Native American children. It is a much-preferred practice to keep the children on the reservation. My daughter and her husband tried and tried to place Willow with a Native American family, but nobody wanted this little girl."

By now Willow had tired of listening to our conversation. She had her shoes off. Her little shirt was red from the drippings of the lollipop in her mouth. She was standing on the seat between her grandparents while they made a circle with their arms so little Willow wouldn't fall. Grandpa and Grandma were worn out. You could see it in their faces.

But, let me tell you, Willow was loved.

"We will teach her everything we can about her heritage. Oh, watch this," Grandma said, as she started beating a tom-tom rhythm on her leg. That little girl, only one and a half years old, started dancing to the beat.

Love can come in strange packages and at inopportune times, but when it comes, the lucky ones are those who choose to embrace it.

Willow Speak Thunder is one lucky little girl! But maybe her new mom, dad, big brothers, and grandparents are the luckiest ones.

For everything there is a season,

and a time for every purpose under heaven.

A time to be born and a time to die . . .

A time to love and a time to hate;

a time of war and a time of peace.

— Ecclesiastes 3: 1,2,8

His Name Was John

It began like a routine day. In the airline industry, "routine day" is an oxymoron. Many things can change the course of our day. This day, it was a mechanical problem with the aircraft.

We'd been up since 4:00 a.m. and by 5:30 were boarding rather sleepy passengers. Most don't say much. They just want to find their seat, get a pillow and blanket, and go back to sleep. Every so often, there's a morning person boarding who is all smiles and chatter. They are the ones we engage in conversation. After all, *we* can't grab a pillow and blanket and go back to sleep.

When the plane was nearly full and boarding was complete, we briefed our emergency exit row, did our safety demo, and buckled ourselves into the jump seats for the ride to Denver. After only a short while taxiing, the plane came to an abrupt halt. A few minutes later, our captain informed us that a "light in the flight deck" needed checking and that we were heading back to our gate. Until a mechanic came on board, we were to remain in the airplane and wait for final word about our departure.

Of course, the sleepy folks were not happy about the news. It's our job to try to make them happy, so we did our best to keep them comfortable, offer water and more pillows, and just wait it out with them.

I had my back to the cabin, talking with the other flight attendants, when I felt a tap on my shoulder. I turned to see a young woman I guessed to be around twenty-five years old standing before me.

"May I talk to you?" she whispered quietly.

"Of course," I said as I took her arm, seating her next to me in one of the empty seats in row one.

The look in her eyes told me something was wrong.

"Hi, I'm Andrea. I'm flying with two friends. We're Marine Corps wives. My friend, Joanna, is asleep by the window."

I looked behind me about four rows and saw her friend. Her head was resting on the window, and she did appear to be asleep. Another friend sat next to Joanna with an arm around her.

"We're flying to Denver and then on to New York City today. See, Joanna's husband was killed in Iraq on Wednesday, and we're going to his funeral. We just *have* to get there today."

My heart sank. My mind raced. *What can I do?*

Andrea's eyes told me she was desperate to find a way to get the three of them to New York *that day*.

The captain informed us that it was going to be a while before we knew the solution to our mechanical problem.

These girls are going to miss their connections to New York, I thought.

"Oh I'm so sorry," was all I could say to Andrea. "Let me see what I can do. Wait here."

Nobody was supposed to leave the aircraft, but I asked the captain if I might take the tickets of these three passengers to the gate agent just inside the jetway door to see if there was something that could be done. He came out of the flight deck and stood by the entry door for me. That allowed me to get off the aircraft.

Nearly half the plane had connecting flights. What would the other passengers think? How could I give these three women special treatment? The gate agent heard my story and set about to do what she could to get them on another flight. I returned to the airplane.

I sat again with Andrea and heard more details.

"We've given her two sleeping pills. We thought we'd be in the air for a couple of hours, and she needs to sleep," Andrea said. "She gets really agitated when she's awake. She is so upset!"

My heart just went out to this poor young woman. I have kids her age. Like most mothers we feel compelled to protect our kids. Tears welled up in my eyes. I quickly brushed them away. I was not going to break down. I needed to be strong.

"John and Joanna were the perfect couple," Andrea continued. "She's beautiful, as you can see, and John was . . . well, he was a hunk. They looked like Ken and Barbie. They got married just a year ago on Valentine's Day."

Valentine's Day. That day always brings happy memories for me. My oldest son, Ross, was born on Valentine's Day.

That day, for Joanna, would have also brought wonderful memories, but now—

Andrea continued, "John was gone just two months. His first tour of duty."

God, WHY? I thought. It's just so unfair. This young couple was just starting their life together. But now no new memories will be made, no children, no growing old together. This realization just tore at my heart.

"She's wearing his Marine Corps sweatshirt. There's comfort in the smell." I guessed it still smelled like his aftershave. "She'll probably never wash it," Andrea said with a sad laugh as she looked away.

Duty called me away for a few moments, and when I walked back I could see Andrea talking to Joanna, who had awakened. She had begun to cry. Her hands held her face as she sobbed.

I leaned over the two friends and touched Joanna for the first time. Again, all I could say was, "I'm so sorry."

The wait was becoming longer and longer. Passengers were getting antsy.

"Will we miss our connections?"

"How much longer?"

"Can't we get off the airplane?"

I tried to get answers, but the mechanics weren't sure yet.

I went to row four and said to Joanna, "Come with me." I took her hand and led her to the front of the aircraft, behind the bulkhead, near the door. I just put my arm around her and held her. She cried. I cried.

"I can't believe this is happening," she repeated over and over. I noticed she held a rosary in her hand and remembered Andrea had said she was really mad at God right now. I understood.

"I know you must feel like you're in a nightmare," I sympathized.

We just stood there, the two of us. Nobody came near. I wanted Joanna to know, somehow, how much I wanted to support her—to "fix" things. How I wished I could change the direction of her life.

Finally the gate agent came on board. She'd pulled some strings, made some phone calls, and somehow managed to get all three women a direct flight from California to New York.

I left Joanna for a moment, got her two friends and all their carry-on items. We deplaned. I'm sure the other passengers wondered why they were allowed off the aircraft. There would be time for explanations later.

I hugged all three women, took a deep breath, wiped the tears from my eyes, and went back to the plane.

God, take care of them, I offered before heading back to work.

As it turned out, they didn't get on the first direct flight, nor the second nor the third. Many factors contributed to that. My crew partners and I didn't know it at the time, but *our* plane wouldn't head for Denver until nearly twelve hours later. Needless to say, we all had some time in the airport.

We three flight attendants kept seeing the three young women as they, too, waited—first at the gate, later riding on an electric cart. Joanna appeared to be doing okay. If nothing else, the delay gave her something to focus on, forcing her to take her mind off the nightmare she was living.

I overheard her talking on a cell phone. "Wednesday? At two? Tell me the name of the church again . . . Please notify everyone . . . It will mean a lot to John." At twenty-five, she was making arrangements to bury the person she had thought would be her life partner. Speaking of him in the past tense would take some time.

Joanna's two friends were there for her, just like she'd have been there for them if the dice had rolled differently. They were *all* military wives.

They finally left that airport on a direct flight to New York City. I learned that they would be met by a military limo and taken to John's parents home in New Jersey.

I never talked with them again. I probably never will. But on the day of the funeral, my thoughts were with them. It must have been torture for Joanna. Fortunately, she had her friends to help carry her through the day as she said her good-bye, one last time, to her young husband John.

I wish I'd had the honor of meeting John. I know I'll never forget Joanna.

The bond that links your true family

is not one of blood,

but of respect and joy in

each other's life.

— Richard Bach

Things Aren't Always What They Seem

"Well hello, little man," I said to the child as he was lifted by his mom into the seat against the window. He appeared to be a man in miniature, dressed in a little button-down shirt and grown-up-style pants. Just as he was seated, I turned to see his dad helping seat an adorable little girl. She was dressed in pink from top to bottom.

"Hi sweetie," I smiled at her. *What a cute family*, I thought.

I didn't see them again until we were serving our in-flight beverages. The kids were well behaved as the parents read to them. *They're such caring parents*, I said to myself. *Good for them.* Too often we see kids behaving badly, and I believe it isn't the kids fault. Lots of love and attention sprinkled with firm discipline works in my book.

As I handed a drink to the mom, my eyes went from the small boy to the little girl and then back again. They looked nothing alike. He was dark-haired; she a little blondie.

"They're twins, right?" I questioned the father, although I didn't really think they were.

"Actually, they're two months apart. But," he added, "they aren't related."

I'm sure my look said *What?* but I just smiled and said, "Oh."

The rest of the drink service was a blur as I wondered. *Not related? Are they adopted? But, why would you adopt them that close together? Are they cousins? Not related.* I just couldn't figure it out.

After we finished our service and collected the trash, I had a few minutes to visit with the couple and their children. Curiosity was really getting to me. I eased into a seat just in front of them. On my knees, I faced them and started to ask questions.

"I'm so curious. If I'm imposing, please just tell me; but how is it that these two darling kids are yours, but not related to each other?"

The young mom looked over at the dad and just smiled. Her look said, *you tell her.* Maybe they were asked these kinds of questions a lot.

"Well, Allysa is my daughter," Jeff started. "Soren is Ashley's son. Ashley and I met just a few months ago."

"Wow!" I said. "How did you meet?" I could tell they enjoyed sharing their unique story.

"Well," continued Jeff, "I was never married to Allysa's mother. Actually, she died."

Things Aren't Always What They Seem

That kind of stopped me for a moment. This little girl doesn't have her mother anymore. She obviously has a very loving, supportive, caring dad though.

Jeff added, "She took her own life."

I was stunned for a moment. I didn't know what to say, so I just continued to listen.

"I was caring for Allysa most of the time anyway. See, her mother suffered from post-partum depression."

I'd heard of that and even had a family member who'd experienced an awful depression after the birth of her first child.

"I left her at a day care near my home while I worked," Jeff continued. "Ashley is the assistant director of the center."

Now it was coming together. Ashley had her son, Soren, at the center, too.

"We became friends." Now it was Ashley adding to the story. "Really good friends. Little Allysa was born on Christmas Day. Soren was born in late October."

Then I asked the question that maybe I shouldn't have. "Are you two married now?" It was none of my business, though they seemed willing to share more.

They looked at each other for a moment, then both blurted at the same time, "Not yet."

I guess I had the answer to my question. Their relationship was unusual, but they seemed to be doing great.

As we flew, the sun set and the cabin darkened. The kids had gotten tired. Ashley was holding Soren in one row. Jeff had moved to the row in front of them. Little Allysa was lying on her tummy with a pillow under her head and a blanket over her tiny body. Her daddy was softly patting her back as she slept.

All I could see was love. They both loved their children and were falling in love with each other and with the other's child.

This is going to work, I smiled to myself.

Just a few minutes prior to landing, Ashley came to the rear of the plane where I was. She slipped into the lavatory. I saw she had a makeup bag and her toothbrush and toothpaste. She'd told me earlier that they were flying to her family's home so her parents could meet Jeff and little Allysa. She was very anxious for everything to be okay.

When she came out of the lavatory, she looked very pretty and very together.

"He seems really nice," I said to her in a girl-to-girl kind of way. I was old enough to be her mother, but some things transcend age.

Her look to me was one of hopefulness and pride and love and excitement, all rolled into one. A big smile spread across her face.

"I think we're going to be a family," was all she had to say.

Some of you say, "Joy is greater than sorrow,"

and others say, "Nay, sorrow is the greater."

But I say unto you, they are inseparable.

Together they come, and when one sits alone

with you at your board, remember that

the other is asleep upon you bed.

— Kahil Gibran

A Time To Live and
A Time To Die

It was about halfway into our flight, a time to rest for a moment after our second beverage service. Tidying up the galley, I stood with my back to the center aisle. Hearing someone approach, I turned around to see the smile of a middle-aged male passenger.

"You don't mind if I stand back here and stretch a bit, do you?" he inquired.

"Not at all," I said. "I could use a little break."

"Sometimes it's hard to stay seated a long time. I had heart surgery some time ago. I just need to get up and move, stretch my legs, get my circulation flowing again," the man explained.

Actually, these exercise sessions are pretty common. Sometimes I laugh when I see people doing elaborate stretching in one of the galleys. People have been warned about sitting still too long for fear they'll get a blood clot and die. That isn't the funny part. It's just that on flights less than an hour in length, I have to wonder if it's necessary to go through such gyrations. How many people get up from their chair in front of the television set every ten minutes to stretch?

But this flight was a long one. I welcomed his company.

"A heart attack?" I asked, assuming that is what he meant by "heart surgery."

"Actually, no," he started. "I'd been having all kinds of heart-related problems. After many, many tests, I was told by my doctor that my heart was dying—I needed a new heart."

What must it feel like to be told that? I thought. *A new heart isn't something you can go to the store and purchase.*

The man continued, "It was awfully scary. I thought of myself and my family first. My wife and kids were quite upset and afraid, of course. But then it hit me. Someone has to die in order for me to live. Now that's a sobering thought."

"Wow, I never thought of that," I said, rather surprised at myself. "How do you go about finding a heart?"

Questions flooded my mind. *Does it have to be a certain size, or age, or blood type?* Luckily the man was comfortable talking about it with me.

"Well, they put your name on a list and then you wait. Some people wait and wait and never find a suitable donor. I was lucky. They found a heart for me in only a few months. It meant I was going to live."

But somebody else had died. Some family was grieving their loss. I didn't know much about him just then, but I knew if I were him I would have wanted to know all the details. *How old was the donor? Were they male or female? Would surgery hurt?*

"The surgery went well. It wasn't bad at all. I was feeling so rotten before surgery, this was a piece of cake!"

A piece of cake? I doubted that, but agreed it was probably not as bad as he expected it to be.

"Did you ever want to find out where your new heart came from?" I sheepishly asked him, really wanting to know.

"You know, I did. That's the best part of my story." A huge smile crossed his face.

"They don't give the recipient the name of the donor, but they do give the name of the recipient to the donor's family." He let that soak in.

"Oh, I see," I said. "The family can then decide if they want to meet the person that received their loved one's heart."

"Exactly," he said.

"Did you find out?" I asked excitedly.

"Yes," he paused for a moment. I could see in his face that finding out who gave him a new chance at life was highly significant.

"After receiving my okay, the hospital gave my name to the donor's family—his wife actually. I learned that my new heart had once beat in the chest of a twenty-five-year-old. That, in itself was exciting, since I'm nearing sixty-five." Another huge smile crossed his face.

"Wow!" I exclaimed. "You really hit the jackpot—a young, healthy man's heart . . . " And then sobering thoughts left me regretting my shortsightedness. The realization suddenly hit me. *That means there's a family that had lost their son—a brother, a friend, a wife, all without this special person in their lives anymore. Such sadness mixed with such joy and promise.*

"Did you ever get to meet the donor's family?"

"Oh, it was wonderful," he said. "My wife and I drove several hours to get to the home of the widow. When we knocked on the door, my knees were banging together, I was so nervous. I didn't know how she'd react. There is just nothing to prepare you for that moment."

I tried to imagine but really couldn't. This young woman was standing face to face with a stranger, but inside his chest beat her husband's heart.

We hugged. She held her ear on my chest for a long moment. I knew what she was doing. We all shared a glass of iced tea and chatted about what kind of man her husband was, about how he was killed. Just as we were about to leave, a small boy came out of the bedroom rubbing his little eyes. 'This is my son,' the woman said. He was a "cutie" about three years old. She held him until he woke up completely, and then, just as we were about to say our good-byes, she whispered something to me. What she said gave me chills . . . and a feeling of being honored.

"She asked, 'Can my little boy sit on your lap? I want him to hear his daddy's heartbeat.'"

We could never learn to be brave

and patient if there were only

joy in the world.

— Helen Keller

Angels Watching Over Me

I was the passenger this time. I didn't have to serve a drink or pick up trash during *this* trip. A good book in hand, I was planning to read during the entire flight. I've heard it said, if you want to make God laugh, tell Him your plans.

A woman about my age slipped into the seat next to me. As she did, we laughed about the tight quarters and long flight. She seemed glad she wasn't sitting alone.

After we were airborne, she and I started to talk. She looked a bit nervous and said, "I'm flying to D.C. to see my daughter. She's just returned from Iraq. She was there twice."

I've wondered many times before how the parents of the kids fighting in a war cope with the worry and stress. I guess they don't have a choice—it is the choice of their child to be there.

"How long has it been since you've seen . . . "

She finished my sentence, "Cori. My daughter's name is Cori."

"Oh, what a pretty name. So how long since you've seen Cori?"

"Nearly a year," she said, her voice cracking.

A year of sitting on pins and needles, I assumed. Every time the news was on, every time the phone rang, there was a moment of fear.

The woman opened up and began telling me about Cori. She'd attended the Naval Academy in Annapolis, Maryland. She was just twenty-eight years old and already an officer.

"I found a tiny, silver angel when I was shopping one day, just before Cori left for Iraq. When we hugged good-bye, I slipped it into her hand and whispered in her ear, 'Keep this in your pocket, Cori. It'll bring you good luck.' For once she didn't say, 'Oh, Mom,' but just put it into her pocket and then left."

I'm sure Cori was as frightened as her mom, but she was an officer and trained to be tough.

"Cori came home after her first tour of duty. One morning at breakfast, she came up and gave me a huge hug. Then she held out her hand. Lying in her palm was that tiny, silver angel. She said, 'I guess it did protect me, Mom. Thanks.'"

Cori's mom and I looked at each other and smiled—the smile of mothers sharing that indescribable bond with their children. She continued, "Cori had to serve another term, so off to Iraq she went. As she left I thought, *She has more experience now . . . and a few more memories of family to carry her through.* And she still had her angel.

"Cori had started having eye problems and had seen an ophthalmologist while she was home. He advised her not to go to Iraq. Something in her eye, anything like dirt and sand, could cause her to lose her eyesight. I begged her not to go, but she's a soldier through and through. She just said, 'I'll be fine, Mom.'"

This story is better than my book, I thought to myself, then realized I had already put it down. I eagerly waited for more of her story.

"Shortly after Cori got to Iraq, she was caught in a sandstorm. A common thing there, but you know, she couldn't afford to have sand in that eye. Don't you know, she damaged her eye and was rushed to a Baghdad hospital. Luckily, her dad and I didn't know about the injury at the time. We worried enough without knowing all the day-to-day details. Baghdad was under fire. What was going to be a quick fix ended up taking several days. Cori told me that she kept her hand in her pocket so she could feel her angel. She really found comfort in the angel."

Just then the captain announced that we were starting our descent into Reagan National Airport. *Boy, the time really flew by,* I laughed to myself. I wanted to hear more about Cori and didn't have much time.

"Cori is actually going to be in her best friend's wedding tomorrow evening. It was touch and go whether or not she'd make it in time. But she's here!" It wouldn't be long and she'd again be face to face with her daughter.

"I did get to talk to her yesterday on the phone. You won't believe what she told me. We knew the fighting had been rough. We didn't know how much danger Cori and the others were in. She said 'Mom, there were three times, seriously, three times that I should not have made it.' Well, *that* was a great comfort," she laughed sarcastically.

Heartstrings at 35,000 Feet • Mary Catherine Carwile

"But," she added, "Cori had her angel, and she just felt protected. When she got on the plane to fly home, she again reached into her pocket for the angel. You know what she found? Her angel had broken in *three* places—but she had all *three pieces*. Three . . . the number of times that she had been in mortal danger."

We both just sat there staring into each other's eyes, lost in our own thoughts—thoughts of God's grace.

I believe the children are our future,

teach them well and let them lead the way.

"Greatest Love Of All"
– Linda Creed and Michael Masser

Protect The Children

We'd just flown in from Minneapolis and were told we'd have to change planes for our continuing flight to San Diego. "It's the ol' bag drag," I said to my fellow flight attendants. Dragging our bags day after day reminds us all that we aren't as young as we used to be.

We could hear a small child's voice as we approached gate thirty-two. We could tell the child was frightened and crying. I wondered what was upsetting her. As I got closer, I saw her. I remember thinking that she couldn't have been more than five years old. She was holding on for dear life to her mother's leg.

"I don't want to go, Mommy," she cried.

The mother was trying to convince this small child that everything was going to be all right. I walked on past them, so I didn't hear her response to the child. I feared she would be on my flight.

Walking down the jetway, I could still hear her sobbing.

"She sure doesn't want to fly today. Wonder what's going on?" I said to the other attendant.

We got busy hoisting our bags into the overhead compartments, checking all the emergency equipment, and getting our galleys ready. The gate agent appeared, saying, "I have a UM and one wheelchair." That's her way of telling me that we have an unaccompanied minor and someone coming down in a wheelchair. I would sign papers for the UM and keep my eye on her until she was handed over to whomever was picking her up in San Diego. I'd also have to order a wheelchair to be waiting in San Diego. Standard stuff.

I didn't think much about the UM until the gate agent brought her down to me at the airplane. It was *her*, the crying, scared little girl I'd seen when we walked through the boarding area.

But she's too little to be flying alone, I thought. *Poor thing.*

Many times I've wondered why people send their children across the country alone. Granted, many of the kids are veterans of this type of travel and seem to know as much as we do about flying. But there are a few that just shouldn't be flying alone. I wish the parents would fly with them. I know it's expensive and it takes time, but the children should be cherished at least that much . . . they're so vulnerable, so trusting.

The gate agent was having trouble walking because the little girl had her arms wrapped around one leg.

"Hi," the agent said to me. "This is Ashlee. She's traveling today to see her daddy." She was trying to be upbeat, but it wasn't working.

"I don't want to go!" the girl wailed again. I could easily tell she wasn't just being a spoiled child. She was *scared*. I wasn't sure just then why.

"Well, hello, Ashlee," I said as I bent down to her level. "Come and sit down. You'll be sitting right up here near me. Do you want to get by the window?"

"*I don't want to go,*" was all she urgently whispered.

I could see I'd have my hands full on this trip. I love flying with the kids, but this was going to be one of those trips that takes an emotional toll.

"How old are you, Ashlee?" I inquired.

"I had a birthday last week," she feebly got out. "I'm six years old."

Six years old? She is a very petite six-year-old, I thought to myself.

I got Ashlee seated and let her look through her small backpack for a stuffed animal she'd packed. It was well worn—her friend, I could tell.

She'd stopped the crying by now but was still sniffling. I tried to distract her by talking with her and showing her around my galley. It proved difficult, as the whole time she had her arms wrapped around *my* legs. *Well, if that gives her comfort, I'll deal with it*, I laughed to myself as I dragged one leg along, heavier by several pounds.

"You're going to see your daddy?" I asked, thinking that would comfort her.

"Last time I saw my daddy I was only two years old," she said. And then she started crying again.

Oh, now I get it, I thought. *She's flying—alone—to see a man everyone calls "her daddy," but she doesn't even know this man. Four years is a lifetime to a small child. Did she have any memory of him? Were they good memories? How long was she going to be with him?*

I wanted to take her off the plane, give her to her mother and tell her how unfair I thought it was to send this little girl all by herself to a man she didn't know, but of course it wasn't my place to say that.

The plane was full by then, and we were about to close the main cabin door. Something inside me welled up. I was mad! I would do all I could to comfort Ashlee on this flight, though I had to remind myself once again that I couldn't save the world.

As soon as the FASTEN SEATBELT sign was turned off, Ashlee got up and joined me in the galley—my little shadow. I let her help serve the beverages. She thought that was great fun. She helped give snacks to everyone on board. The other passengers were delighted to be served by this little, fellow passenger and with her mind off her fear, she was having a ball.

But, all too soon the FASTEN SEATBELT sign came on again. We were beginning our descent into San Diego. I got Ashlee back to her seat, buckled her in, and told her we were almost there.

Ashlee's tears started again. As I sat down on the jump seat and strapped myself in, I was at it again—wasting mental energy with impossible requests. *God, I wish I could take away her fear. She's growing up too fast, and she's learning to tough it out by herself. Those are things we have to learn . . . but she's only six years old.*

When we landed and everyone had deplaned, I took Ashlee up the jetway. She was still clinging to my leg. I saw a man looking toward the door, searching for someone. He saw her first.

"Ashlee!" he yelled. "Look how big you've gotten."

I was delighted that he appeared to be a nice man. He was well dressed, didn't smell of alcohol, and seemed anxious to hug his little girl. Why it had been four years since he'd seen her didn't seem to matter at this point. My job was to deliver Ashlee to her dad. I said a prayer of thanks that it turned out to be easier than I had thought it would be.

I walked slowly back down the jetway fighting back tears, until I heard her scream my name. Just as I turned, she almost knocked me over, wrapping her arms around my legs one last time. Then to my relief, Ashlee looked up at me, smiled, let go of my leg and rejoined her dad.

It looks like Ashlee is going to be all right, I thought.

At least this ending was a happy one. Memories of other, not-so-happy endings flooded my mind. I remembered a boy about eight years old. He, too, was crying in the gate area. He, too, was being told by his mother that he'd be okay. He, too, was going to see his dad.

That young man was sullen throughout the flight. He was trying to be brave, but clearly he did not want to be going on this cross-country trip to see his dad.

It all became clear when I handed him over at the gate. We had to wait several minutes because the father wasn't there. *Not a good sign*, I remembered thinking.

As the dad walked toward us, I could smell him. He reeked of alcohol and wasn't walking too well either.

"Hey," he said rather loudly, "there you are, kid. I hear you were a big cry baby on the plane . . . "

My heart skipped a beat. I handed him the signed form; I smiled feebly, and the two of them walked away from me.

It isn't always easy in life for kids or adults. There are tough times for us all. But that is no reason for excusing ourselves from the real responsibility of parenthood—cherishing our child. Pearl S. Buck wrote, "If our American way of life fails the child, it fails us all."

Grow old along with me!

The best is yet to be,

The last of life, for which the first was made:

.   .   .   .

So fall asleep love, loved by me . . . for I know love,

I am loved by thee.

— Robert Browning

Precious Cargo:
The Rest of The Story

It's fun to go back and retrace the moment—the first look, the first conversation, the first feeling that we've met someone special. It had all started on Saturday. It was a long flight from Florida to Denver. We'd just started flying to this Florida city, so the plane wasn't very full. The flight left early in the morning. Maybe that's why so few had chosen to fly.

The man walked toward me. I was standing in my usual spot for boarding, the exit row. There's just a bit more leg room for the passengers, and it gives me room to stand while greeting passengers.

"Well, here's the kind of guy I like to see in my exit row," I said to him. Looking back, I think, *Oh, now that was an intelligent remark.* But right then, he was just another passenger and I was just making friendly small talk.

The boarding process went fast that morning. There were several young moms with babies and kids in tow. I love talking with the children. They're always so excited to be in an airplane!

As we began our beverage service, I found myself at the exit row again. I asked the man if I could get him a beverage. *What a smile he has,* I said to myself. Something inside me stirred.

Finding myself intrigued by this very handsome gentleman, I made my way back to the exit row. We began chatting. Our conversation came so easily. I inquired about why he was flying to Denver, and he told me he lived there. When he said he was a writer, I wanted to hear all about it. My oldest son writes, and I had a lot of questions. We exchanged telephone numbers so that he and my son could connect. I secretly hoped he'd call *me!*

Every time I returned to the galley in the back of the plane, I had a smile on my face, and every time it was bigger than before.

"I don't know what it is about him," I said to my fellow attendant. But there was *something.*

When we landed in Denver, the passengers deplaned. *Mr. Exit Row* shook my hand, said, "I'll call," and was gone.

I said a silent prayer that I'd hear from him soon.

Funny, no matter your age, matters of the heart can reduce you to a nervous teenager!

The next day, Sunday, was a busy one for me. I'd left my cell phone in my car the entire day since I wouldn't have been able to answer it anyway. I was finally able to turn it on at nearly seven that night, and the message on my phone read TWO NEW MESSAGES. Pressing the LISTEN button, I heard his voice. Butterflies came alive in my stomach. He called! And he wanted to have dinner with me the next night.

I returned his call, and he asked again if I was available for dinner the following evening.

"Well, yes," I started, "but it'll have to be later. See, tomorrow I'm flying to San Francisco to pick up a five-month-old, newly adopted Korean baby. I'll fly him back to Denver and hand him over to his new mom and dad. So, yes, I'd love to have dinner. Can you wait until seven thirty or so?"

There was silence on the other end of the line. Then he said, "Tell me what you're doing again."

I explained again how I was escorting a baby from San Francisco to Denver.

After a long pause he asked, "Can I ask you something? Would you mind if I come to the airport and watch you?"

What? I thought. "You want to drive all the way to the airport, park, and then walk all that way just to watch me?" I asked. That's when he had me. There's no doubt about it.

"Well, if you don't mind. I think that's the nicest thing I've ever heard about anyone doing," he quietly said.

While I was flying home from San Francisco with little Owen asleep in my arms, the man of my dreams was driving to Denver International Airport, parking his car, and making his way to the meeting place where I'd deliver a precious gift to the new parents.

He got there with about a half hour to spare. He was there alone—except for a young couple and five others. They all held blue balloons. He guessed correctly that they were the new parents, grandparents, and friends.

"Any chance you're waiting for someone named Mary?" he asked them.

"Oh my god! Do you know her? She's bringing us our baby!" the new mom shrieked.

With that, my new "Mr. Wonderful" became Uncle Ernie. They shared with him their excitement, then handed him their video camera.

"Would you mind?" they asked.

He couldn't have been happier or more excited. They all waited together until they saw the baby and me come into view.

Ernie told me later, "When I saw the look on your face as you gave that precious baby to his new parents—well that was it. That's when you had me."

That's how simply and beautifully it happened. We were married a year and a half later.

I often remember my tiny silver fork, engraved with "The Best Is Yet To Come"—and I smile.

If we were to wake up some morning and find
that everyone was the same race, creed and
color, we would find some other cause for
prejudice by noon.

– George Aiken

A Rose Is a Rose

Sometimes a passenger's plight just reaches inside me and grabs something.

I'd seen the young man board. He was being assisted to the aircraft by the gate agent. He was a tall, handsome teenager, probably about sixteen years old. He didn't have any apparent physical problems, and if there were any mental problems I sure couldn't detect any. I wondered why he was being assisted. Before I had time to give it much thought, he was down the aisle and in his assigned seat.

Every time I passed by him, our eyes locked on each other. His eyes seemed to say, "Get me outta here. Please!"

I was fortunate on this flight that I had time to sit with him on a couple of occasions. Even though we were interrupted several times throughout the duration of the flight, I heard his story.

"Mom and Dad are sending me to stay with my older brother for a while," he started. It seemed things were not going according to his parent's plan. Apparently, he was not becoming the kind of son they had always imagined he'd be.

At first, I didn't quite get what he was talking about. The teenage years can be a trying time for parents, I know. I've heard it said we should send kids away when they are twelve and get them back when they are twenty. God blessed me with two sons who had been relatively "un-trying" during their teen years, and I've always felt fortunate.

After we'd talked awhile, I felt that he was getting comfortable and that he was open to sharing something with me. I became more at ease in asking him more questions.

"Are you in trouble at school," I asked him.

"No, not at all. I'm an 'A' student, actually," he smiled proudly.

What a nice kid, I thought. *What in the world is going on?*

"I guess they think that my brother can straighten me out."

The sarcastic way he emphasized the word 'straighten' made me understand, then, what he was talking about. This young man had come to realize that he was gay, and his parents were sending him away. They hoped he'd come home "fixed," and their lives would once again be "normal."

I felt such empathy for this young man. I put my arm around him. He didn't resist at all.

"Sweetheart," I started, "you are perfect, just the way you are. A tiger can't change his stripes, nor can anybody do it for him. Don't let anyone tell you that you are something you are not. There are resources to help you understand about yourself. There are support groups for your parents."

We stayed in our little hug for several moments. When I pulled away, I saw that his face was wet with tears. My heart

A Rose Is A Rose

went out to him again, and I wished there was a way I could speak to his parents, his brother.

The way I see it, God makes all of us. We are all different. Every one of us is unique. A rose is a rose is a rose. No amount of praying, wishing, hoping, dreaming—or therapy—will make a rose a tulip. And we must remember, even the rose has thorns; it isn't all painless perfection.

We were about to land, and I had my preparatory work to do. I left my new friend hoping he felt better than when he'd boarded the plane.

When I opened the main cabin door, his brother was waiting just outside. He'd been able to get permission to meet the plane. One would have thought that he was meeting a prisoner, that this young man was going to hurt someone. Perhaps they thought he'd flee—my heart almost wished he would.

"Hey, Buddy," shouted his older brother. They hugged the way insecure men hug—awkwardly, quickly, ending with a slap or two on the back and a turning of the head to avoid eye contact. His brother was trying so hard to project masculinity. I just knew the future was going to be very hard for this young man.

"Take care of yourself," I called after him. *And God, You take care of him too,* I prayed.

In several of the accounts in this book, I mention
the piece written by my son, Ross.

For those of you who might be wondering about
this piece, I share it here with you.

It was given to me on a Mother's Day
some years ago, and I cherish it.

Ross's Story: You Knew

Somewhere in those first weeks, the tiny heartbeat started its pulse and you knew. Inside you there were two rhythms. And for those months, though their cadence was not always synchronized, dual hearts beat in one body.

You knew my name before my fingers were formed, before my backbone unfurled, before my first rustlings in your womb opened your eyes wide and brimmed them over with fear and wonder. You knew later that your pains were too early and that you should be frightened.

What were your thoughts during your swells of contraction and the glare of hospital lights and uncertainty? A young woman's heartbreak at the unthinkable advice offered her by the doctors—to not call anybody with the news, just yet. Your heart, now separate but forever linked with your son's, must have hammered behind your ribs as you were taken to see me for the first time, and how it must have been soothed when the infant eyes that met yours told you that all was going to be well and good. You told yourself that this was something you already knew.

Strapped for energy and money years later, with enterprising hopes and a second child, you gratefully accepted the chance for a break. Smooth talk by a villain in a position of trust, along with your fatigue, may have clouded your vision. But when my eyes, a bit older by then, couldn't meet yours as you sensed a wrong was being done to me, you knew.

You knew also to handle familial hardships with tact. Never once did you throw in our faces the grime from the toilets you scrubbed at midnight to build your business. Never did you speak badly about the man that had betrayed your trust and left you . . . because that man is our father. You never asked us to comfort you because you realized that we needed you to appear strong. You cried alone in a borrowed home with a struggling business, a thin wallet, and the responsibility of raising two young boys into gentlemen.

And again, you looked into the eyes of your firstborn and then asked me a question you didn't want to ask. And my answer was one you didn't want to hear. But through your tears and disappointment, your heart swelled with love, and you believed you would grow to understand. You held me while my own fears racked my body with sobs, and you whispered comfort and the words, "I knew, Ross."

On this day, Mother's Day, you remain the most powerful and positive force in my life. You have done what mothers are all-too-rarely able to do: earned and retained the respect and reverence of her child. My heart and mind, literally only existing through you, grow continually stronger and more enlightened by your influence. And I will keep telling you, time after time . . . even if you already know.

No Ordinary Day

It started out as any ordinary day, rather monotonous, the same routine just different people. Little did I know how suddenly the world would turn upside down with me caught in a vortex.

The woman was upset—very upset. When she approached me it was clear she was ill. Her eyes were hollow, frightened. She wanted to talk. She *needed* to talk. Asking me to sit down next to her, with tears streaming down her cheeks, she began.

"I am not going to make it to my son's birthday. My doctor told me I have just a few months to live. I am so scared."

To be continued . . .

Mary Catherine Carwile is working on her second book, *More Heartstrings*. To view an excerpt and order her book go to *www.marycarwile.com* or call 720.488.3196.